- Don't sell for under 6 figures — be insulted
  - you have gross sales of $150K
- Don't accept for under 6 figures
  - how much they invest in you = how much they are invested in the success of your work
- This editor knows what he's doing. It's his job to "get" you for as low as possible.
- Would you sell [illegible] for $10K?
- Editor is taking advantage of you. He is appealing to your [illegible] side, this is not [illegible]. "To prosper," and when you win the Oscar, they will own you for pennies on the dollar.
- "I have ~~stuff that tell~~ [illegible]."

Hey! Hi! Hey buddy hi! Hello! Hoo hoo! Heyhibuddy!